Forests

To the One who created forests.

—*Genesis* 1:11–12

Published by
PEACHTREE PUBLISHERS
1700 Chattahoochee Avenue
Atlanta, Georgia 30318-2112
www.peachtree-online.com

Illustrations created in watercolor on archival quality 100% rag watercolor paper.
Text and titles set in Novarese from Adobe.

Printed in November 2013 by Imago in Singapore
10 9 8 7 6 5 4 3 2 1
First Edition

Library of Congress Cataloging-in-Publication Data

Sill, Cathryn P., 1953- author.
  About habitats : forests / Cathryn Sill ; illustrated by John Sill.
     pages cm. – (About habitats)
  Audience: Ages 2 to 6.
  Audience: K to grade 3.
ISBN: 978-1-56145-734-2 / 1-56145-734-5
  1. Forest ecology—Juvenile literature. 2. Forests and forestry—Juvenile literature. 3.
Forest animals—Juvenile literature. I. Sill, John, illustrator. II. Title. III. Title: Forests.
IV. Series: Sill, Cathryn P., 1953- About habitats.
  QH541.5.F6S55 2014
  577.3—dc23
                           2013026215

ABOUT HABITATS

Forests

Written by **Cathryn Sill**   Illustrated by **John Sill**

PEACHTREE
ATLANTA

MAJOR FOREST AREAS OF THE WORLD

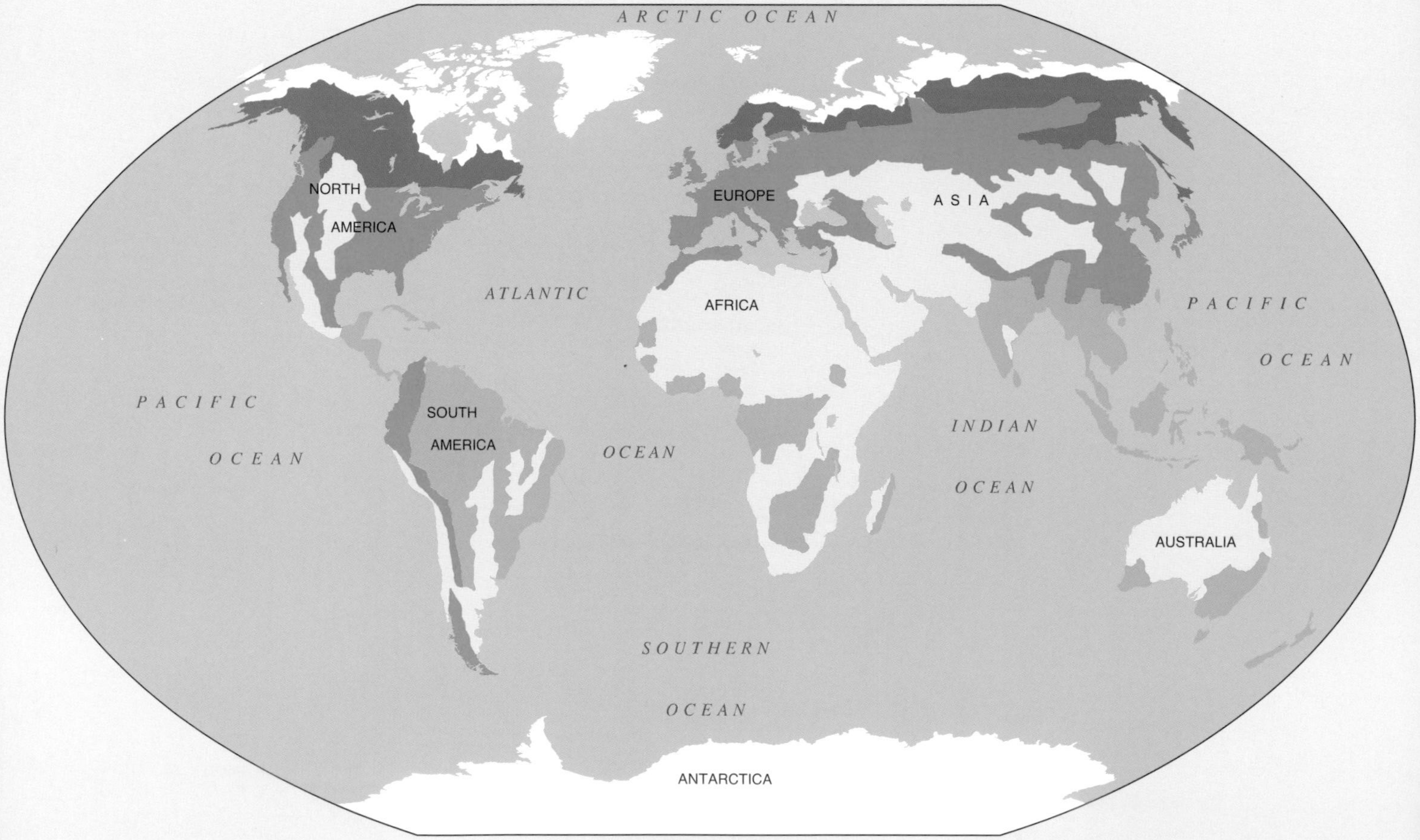

ARCTIC OCEAN

NORTH
AMERICA

EUROPE

ASIA

ATLANTIC

AFRICA

PACIFIC

OCEAN

PACIFIC

SOUTH
AMERICA

OCEAN

INDIAN

OCEAN

OCEAN

AUSTRALIA

SOUTHERN

OCEAN

ANTARCTICA

LEGEND
- Boreal Forests
- Temperate Forests
- Tropical Forests

PLEASE NOTE: Map and forest areas are not to scale.

Forests

Forests are large areas of land covered with many trees.

The trees and other plants in forests
are different sizes and grow in layers.

PLATE 2
TROPICAL RAINFOREST

Tall trees make up the top layer, which is called the canopy.

PLATE 3
CLOUD FOREST

Resplendent Quetzal

Smaller trees and bushes grow in the middle layer, which is called the understory.

Fungi and small plants grow on the forest floor.

Some forests have four different seasons each year.

Most trees that grow in forests with four seasons drop their leaves in autumn.

PLATE 7
DECIDUOUS FOREST

European Bison

European Birch

Some forests are very cold much of the year.

Most trees that live in cold forests have special leaves called needles.

Plate 9
BOREAL FOREST

Siberian Jay

White Spruce

Some forests have warm weather all the time. Many warm forests get a lot of rainfall year-round.

Other warm forests have a wet season
and a dry season.

PLATE 11
TROPICAL DRY FOREST

Keel-billed Toucan

Many animals find food and shelter in forests.

PLATE 12
DECIDUOUS FOREST

Background:
  Black Bear
  Broad-winged Hawk
  Brown Creeper

Foreground:
  Question Mark Butterfly
  Red-spotted Salamander
  Box Turtle

Some animals live in trees.

PLATE 13
TROPICAL RAINFOREST

Green Tree Python

Other forest animals live on the ground under the trees.

Forests help keep much of Earth's fresh water clean and pure.

They provide many things people use.

PLATE 16

a) chocolate
b) medicine
c) wood products
d) paper products

a.

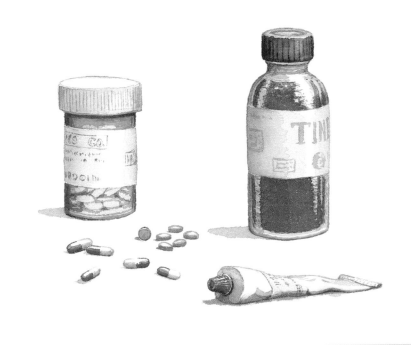

b.

c.

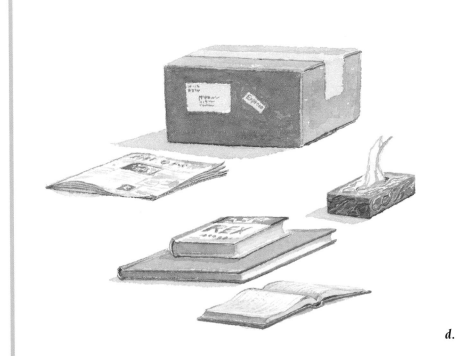

d.

Forests are important places that need to be protected.

Afterword

PLATE 1

Forests are found in places where there is enough warm weather and water for trees to grow. About one-third of Earth's land is covered with forests. Boreal forests are the largest forests in the world. They are made up of coniferous trees such as spruces, pines, and larches. Gray Wolves live in boreal forests as well as other habitats. They used to range over most of the northern hemisphere, but they now live only in a few areas in North America and Eurasia.

PLATE 2

Different kinds of plants grow in each forest layer. The three main layers are the forest floor, the understory, and the canopy. Tropical forests often have a fourth one called the emergent layer. It is made up of the tallest trees that grow above the canopy.

PLATE 3

The tall branches of the forest canopy get the most sunlight. This causes the canopy to grow into a thick covering that shades the plants lower down. Many plants and animals live in the forest canopy. The branches in cloud forest canopies are often covered with special plants called epiphytes, which get their water and nutrients from the air instead of the soil. Resplendent Quetzals live in mountain forests in Central America and northern South America.

PLATE 4

The trees and bushes of the understory do not get as much sunlight as the canopy. Young trees grow slowly in the dim light until a larger tree falls and makes an opening, allowing in more light. The extra light helps them grow taller and become part of the canopy. Smaller trees and bushes that grow well in the shade live under the larger trees. Varied Thrushes are found in the understory of the temperate rainforest in northwestern North America.

PLATE 5

Many plants found on the floor of deciduous forests grow and bloom in early spring before the tree leaves shade the ground. This allows them to get the most sunlight during their growing season. Mosses are small plants that live in damp shady places such as the forest floor. Fungi are living things similar to plants, but they have no flowers or leaves. Eastern Chipmunks are small ground squirrels that live in deciduous forests of eastern North America.

PLATE 6

Deciduous forests with four seasons each year are found in the temperate areas of the world, where the weather is not very hot and not very cold. Warm summers, fairly short winters, and plenty of rainfall help deciduous forests grow.

PLATE 7
The leaves of deciduous trees change color and drop in autumn. Trees stop growing during the winter. Warmer spring weather causes them to start growing again, and new leaves begin to appear. During summer the trees continue to grow. European Bison are forest animals that used to live throughout Europe. They became extinct in the wild because they were overhunted and their forest homes were cleared. European Bison have been returned to a few places in Eastern Europe.

PLATE 8
Boreal forests (also called "taiga") are the world's largest forests. Since winters there can last up to eight months, growing seasons in boreal forests are very short. Winter temperatures can sometimes fall below -50° F (-46° C). Boreal forests stretch across the northern parts of North America and Eurasia. Snowshoe Hares live in boreal forests of North America. These animals are named for their large feet, which help them move around over the deep snow.

PLATE 9
Most of the trees that grow in boreal forests are conifers. Many conifers are evergreen—their needles stay on all year. They grow hard scaly cones to hold their seeds. Coniferous trees have pointed tops and wide bottoms that allow the snow to slide off. This keeps the branches from breaking under the weight of heavy snow. Siberian Jays live year-round in boreal forests in Eurasia. They store food for winter by sticking it in the cracks of tree bark.

PLATE 10

Tropical forests grow in the warm areas near Earth's equator. The abundant rainfall in tropical rainforests helps many plants grow. Some scientists believe that more than half of the world's plants and animals live in tropical rainforests. Orangutans live in rainforests in Southeast Asia. They build nests in trees and sometimes use large leaves as umbrellas.

PLATE 11

Not all tropical forests have rain year-round. Many trees in tropical dry forests lose their leaves during the dry season. Keel-billed Toucans live in tropical forests in Central and northern South America. In dry forests these birds are usually found near rivers and streams.

PLATE 12

Many of the animals that live in forests are not easily seen. They may be high in the branches of the canopy, camouflaged against tree bark, hidden on the forest floor, or buried under the ground. Black Bears, Broad-winged Hawks, Brown Creepers, Box Turtles, Question Mark Butterflies, and Red-spotted Salamanders live in deciduous forests in eastern North America.

PLATE 13

Some animals that live in trees never move down to the forest floor. Other tree-dwelling animals such as Green Tree Pythons sometimes come to the ground to hunt for food. They rest in trees by looping their bodies over a branch and placing their heads in the middle of the coil. Green Tree Pythons live in tropical forests of Indonesia, Papua New Guinea, and northern Australia.

PLATE 14

Though forest floors are usually dark and damp, many animals live and hunt for food there. Some animals, including insects and worms, eat the dead plants that have fallen to the ground. Leafcutter Ants take pieces of leaves to their underground homes, chew them up, and store them there. A fungus grows on the chewed leaves, providing food for the ants. White-nosed Coatis eat insects, small animals, and fruit. Leafcutter Ants and White-nosed Coatis live in North, Central, and South America. Strawberry Poison Dart Frogs eat ants and mites. They live in parts of Central America.

PLATE 15

Forests help clean and store much of Earth's fresh water. Trees help water from rain and snow soak slowly into the ground. The forest soil filters pollutants and slowly releases the water to streams, rivers, and underground wells. Plants in forests help protect the land from floods and mudslides. Northern River Otters live in lakes, rivers, and streams in parts of North America.

PLATE 16

Many people around the world live and work in forests. Forests provide people with various types of foods, including fruits, nuts, and meat from game animals. Some medicines are made from forest plants. Wood from trees is an important material for building and the production of paper.

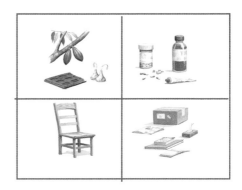

PLATE 17

Much forestland is in danger because too many trees are being cut down. Forests are cleared for farming as well as for wood products. Well-managed forests provide sustainable resources that are used to benefit people and the environment. When a tree is planted for every tree that is cut down, the amount of forested land can remain the same. Ivory-billed Woodpeckers used to live in mature bottomland forests in southeastern North America. Many scientists believe that these large woodpeckers are now extinct because of habitat destruction.

GLOSSARY

BIOME—an area such as a forest or wetland that shares the same types of plants and animals

ECOSYSTEM—a community of living things and their environment

HABITAT—the place where animals and plants live

Boreal—found or growing in the northern part of the world

Cloud forest—a tropical or subtropical mountain forest that is often covered by clouds

Cone—the fruit of a coniferous tree

Coniferous—referring to trees or bushes that hold their seeds in cones

Deciduous—referring to plants that drop all their leaves yearly

Epiphyte—a type of plant that lives on the branches or trunks of other plants

Equator—an imaginary line around the center of the earth halfway between the North and South Poles

Evergreen—referring to plants that have needles or leaves all year long

Northern hemisphere—the half of Earth above the equator

Temperate—not very hot and not very cold

Tropical—hot year-round

BIBLIOGRAPHY

BOOKS

CONIFEROUS FORESTS by Donna Latham (Nomad Press)

DECIDUOUS FORESTS by Donna Latham (Nomad Press)

EARTH MATTERS edited by David Rothschild (DK Publishing)

EYE WONDER: FOREST by Deborah Lock & Lorrie Mack (DK Publishing)

RAINFORESTS by James Harrison (Kingfisher)

WEBSITES

http://www.mbgnet.net/

http://www.thewildclassroom.com/biomes/index.html

http://www.discovertheforest.org/

ISBN 978-1-56145-234-7 HC
ISBN 978-1-56145-312-2 PB

ISBN 978-1-56145-038-1 HC
ISBN 978-1-56145-364-1 PB

ISBN 978-1-56145-688-8 HC
ISBN 978-1-56145-699-4 PB

ISBN 978-1-56145-301-6 HC
ISBN 978-1-56145-405-1 PB

ISBN 978-1-56145-256-9 HC
ISBN 978-1-56145-335-1 PB

ISBN 978-1-56145-588-1 HC

ISBN 978-1-56145-207-1 HC
ISBN 978-1-56145-232-3 PB

ISBN 978-1-56145-141-8 HC
ISBN 978-1-56145-174-6 PB

ISBN 978-1-56145-358-0 HC
ISBN 978-1-56145-407-5 PB

ISBN 978-1-56145-331-3 HC
ISBN 978-1-56145-406-8 PB

ISBN 978-1-56145-743-4 HC
ISBN 978-1-56145-741-0 PB

ISBN 978-1-56145-536-2 HC

ISBN 978-1-56145-183-8 HC
ISBN 978-1-56145-233-0 PB

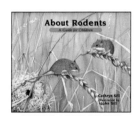

ISBN 978-1-56145-454-9 HC

ABOUT HABITATS SERIES

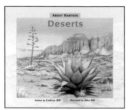

ISBN 978-1-56145-641-3 HC
ISBN 978-1-56145-636-9 PB

ISBN 978-1-56145-559-1 HC

ISBN 978-1-56145-469-3 HC
ISBN 978-1-56145-731-1 PB

ISBN 978-1-56145-432-7 HC
ISBN 978-1-56145-689-5 PB

ISBN 978-1-56145-618-5 HC

ISBN 978-1-56145-734-2 HC

THE SILLS

Cathryn Sill, a former elementary school teacher, is the author of the acclaimed ABOUT… and the ABOUT HABITATS series. With her husband John and brother-in-law Ben Sill, she coauthored three popular bird-guide parodies, including the new edition of A FIELD GUIDE TO LITTLE-KNOWN AND SELDOM-SEEN BIRDS OF NORTH AMERICA.

John Sill is a prize-winning and widely published wildlife artist who illustrates both the ABOUT… and the ABOUT HABITATS series. He also illustrated and coauthored the field guide parodies. A native of North Carolina, he holds a B.S. in wildlife biology from North Carolina State University.

The Sills live in North Carolina.